John Pritchard was Bishop of Oxford until his retirement in 2014. He was formerly Bishop of Jarrow and, before that, Archdeacon of Canterbury. He has served in parishes in Birmingham and Taunton, and has been Diocesan Youth Officer for Bath and Wells diocese. Other books by the author include *The Intercessions Handbook, Beginning Again, How to Pray, Living Easter Through the Year, How to Explain Your Faith, The Life and Work of a Priest, Going to Church* and *Living Jesus.* He is married to Wendy and has two married daughters.

Little Books of Guidance
Finding answers to life's big questions!

Also in the series:

WHY GO TO CHURCH?

A little book of guidance

JOHN PRITCHARD

First published in Great Britain in 2015

Society for Promoting Christian Knowledge
36 Causton Street
London SW1P 4ST
www.spck.org.uk

British Library Cataloguing-in-Publication Data
A catalogue record for this book is available from the British Library

ISBN 978–0–281–07441–9
eBook ISBN 978–0–281–07445–7

Typeset by Graphicraft Limited, Hong Kong
First printed in Great Britain by Ashford Colour Press
Subsequently digitally printed in Great Britain

eBook by Graphicraft Limited, Hong Kong

Produced on paper from sustainable forests

Contents

Introduction

There's an old story about a mother who went to wake up her son one Sunday morning. 'Come on now,' she said, 'time to get up and go to church.' The son moaned loudly. 'I don't want to go to church,' he said. 'Come on,' she coaxed soothingly, 'you know we go to church on Sunday morning.' 'Why should I?' he said. 'They don't like me and I don't like them.' 'Well – two reasons,' said his mother; 'first, you're 42 years old, and second, you're the vicar!'

Sometimes even regular churchgoers wonder if there isn't something more enjoyable to do than struggle out of bed, organize the children, get the lunch on, drive to church, and then sit through 80 minutes of substandard worship full of minor irritations, only to emerge frazzled and frustrated after weak coffee and soft biscuits, having lost one child and nearly lost one's temper. Wouldn't it be easier to be a contented non-believer? Wouldn't a lie-in, brunch and the Sunday newspapers be a better preparation for the coming week?

This little book is for people wondering whether to keep going to church and for those who are wondering whether to try it. These days going to church is much more a decision than a convention. I want to argue that it's worth it. I want to be honest about the problems but confident about the value.

I'm trying, in a fairly random way, to offer a number of answers to the question 'Why go to church?' I don't want to underestimate the difficulties and so I attempt to stand with the sceptics as well as the faithful. But whenever I identify the problems, I hope it will be seen that I do so affectionately. I love the Church, which has brought me great pleasure, deep friendships, much intellectual stimulation and above all, the huge privilege of knowing God.

1

Reasons for not going to church

Until a few years ago, Christians could be a bit smug about people who didn't go to church. They could say it was a bit like not having a wash – the excuses for not doing so were pretty feeble. 'I was made to wash as a child.' 'I just don't have time to wash these days.' 'I used to wash but it got boring so I stopped.' 'I still wash on special occasions like Christmas and Easter.' 'None of my friends wash.' 'People who make soap are only after your money.' 'The bathroom's never warm enough' (I have sympathy with that one).

Now, however, this self-satisfied approach seems outdated and simplistic. There are lots of good reasons for not going to church. Indeed, the boot is on the other foot. Why *would* ordinary, decent, reasonable people disrupt family life on a Sunday morning to attend church? Let's look at the problems. I won't spare the critique – we have to face popular misgivings squarely and honestly. But I don't accept that this is all that can be said, of course; that's what the rest of the book is about!

'I don't believe in God'

Not believing in God seems pretty rock solid as a reason for staying in bed on Sunday morning. Worshipping a God you don't believe in would seem to be a curious use of time, on a par with leaving messages in the fireplace for Father Christmas, or looking out for low-flying storks when a baby is due. On the other hand, this reason for not going to church has to be used with care because you just never know . . . There are very good intellectual reasons for believing in God, and it's worth having an honest look. In any case, the passing years have a strange way of reversing your youthful convictions (as in 'It's all downhill after 40' or 'My parents don't understand a thing'). Sometimes these about-turns are of major proportions. The world-famous philosopher Antony Flew had made quite a name for himself as an outspoken atheist until, in later life, he became convinced of the reality and necessity of God. He came to believe that the only good explanation of the origin of life and the complexity of nature is a Supreme Intelligence. It's a 'conversion' that can leave no atheist untroubled.[1]

'The Church is a hierarchical, controlling institution in an age of freedom and choice'

In other words, the Church as a whole is one of those oppressive institutions we began to throw off in the 1960s and whose agonizing demise we've been watching ever since. It's simply not fit for purpose in handling our spiritual needs. Bono of the band U2 once said: 'I'm not into religion. I'm completely anti-religious. Religion is a term for a collection, a denomination. I am interested in personal experience of God.' (Interestingly, Bono has since found churches to be essential partners in his humanitarian campaigns and says, sheepishly: 'I'm starting to like these church people.') To many people the Church controls and restricts human freedom. Its rigidity, both in doctrine and morality, means that it takes up conservative stances on ethical issues and seeks to impose those views on society at large. The Church is out of touch, out of time and out of favour. Why would I join it?

'I used to go, but . . .'

How often does a priest or pastor hear that line? There are still huge numbers of people in our society who used to go to church but stopped when they got to secondary school because nobody else went any more; or they moved house and somehow never got linked up with a new church; or they got caught up in a church row and said they'd never darken the doors again; or they fell out with the vicar; or they were overworked in church and swore never to get involved again; or they got divorced and felt misunderstood. The reasons are legion.

Family life got too complex with all the demands on those precious weekends which turn out to be the only family space left – this is a genuine dilemma. Or maybe the church was too conservative/became too charismatic/gave me no help with my depression, bereavement, unemployment – it goes on. Saddest of all, perhaps, is the charge that someone had honest questions and doubts and couldn't find any way of raising them or having them dealt with in an adult fashion, so that belief became less and less persuasive and he or she drifted into agnosticism.

'I just don't see the point'

Ah! Tricky. Without some touch of the Divine Magician, some intimation of immortality, some whisper from a strange land, it's hard to see what going to church has got, that going out for the day, having a long pub lunch or dozing in the garden hasn't got. You can't manufacture divine longing. In any case, many people find that their spiritual needs are met through climbing mountains or listening to music. On the other hand, a Christian is entitled to wonder whether people always listen closely enough to that whisper in the night, that desire to say 'Thank you', that disturbing shift in the internal landscape. There may be an alternative narrative after all . . .

'The services are dire'

This reason for not going to church is a humdinger. It takes any number of forms, all of which, on a bad day, I have experienced. Hymns are squeezed out of a terminally ill organ or brutally murdered by what used to be called a choir. A contemporary variation is the music group singing fervently but with an Olympian disregard for the embarrassment of the congregation, particularly the men. The readings are utterly obscure, and the prayers are alternately tedious and off the wall. The sermon is naïve to the point of parody and shows no awareness of the contemporary world, the subtlety of biblical interpretation, or the fact that Edna Bucket is snoring loudly. Follow this up with what is fondly called 'fellowship over coffee' but which, for the newcomer, is more like an exercise in exclusion, and you have to wonder why people are surprised that their church doesn't grow.

A young woman went to church for the first time since her baptism 20 years before. She said afterwards that she wouldn't be going again, and handed her churchgoing friend a list which read:

> You are asking me to change the way I speak, the sort of music I enjoy, the length of time I usually listen to a speaker, the type of people I mix with, my body temperature, the type of chair I sit on, the type of clothes I'm used to seeing people wear, my sense of humour. You expect me to know when to stand, sit and kneel. I am prepared to change, but there was nowhere I could connect any part of my life with that service.

Ouch! But speak of change and the atmosphere can get distinctly chilly. A verger once observed to a visiting bishop: 'It's only inertia that keeps this place going!'

Sunday worship is still the shop window of the Church. It has the power to convert or to repel. For all that churchgoers say worship is an encounter with God and requires engagement from everyone present, and that it's not just

Christian entertainment, the Church still has to make sure that its worship is designed and offered to the highest standard it can possibly manage. What is being offered has to be the genuine article.

'The building is cold and forbidding'

It's hard to do much about this problem, at least in the short term. Churches are hugely expensive to run and even more expensive to adapt. Sometimes it seems as if the interior design is by Stalin, heating by the Arctic Refrigeration Co., lighting by Gloom and Sons, and soft furnishings by the prison service. Enter a church and you've stepped back 50 years in terms of contemporary design. Do you remember when high-street banks were built to look strong and secure, with marble pillars and large, impressive halls? Now we have friendly, intimate, carpeted 'shops', with customer service personnel and coffee. But churches have proved more complex to adapt.

Part of their glory is their 'otherness'. The Church of England alone has 16,000 churches, 13,000 of which are listed and among the most significant buildings historically and architecturally in the country. They may need toilets, kitchen facilities, new heating, lighting, and sound amplification systems. Pews require the congregation to sit in serried ranks, as in old-fashioned classrooms, unable to see more than the back of someone's head. They assume a uni-directional mode of communication, and that God is located somewhere beyond the east wall. The back of the church may look like the remains of a jumble sale, with sad piles of leaflets advertising last month's events, and stacks of battered books announcing that God is prayed to in language of the seventeenth century and sung to in language of the nineteenth.

The cumulative message of this kind of church can be fairly formidable – 'Don't interfere; you're here under sufferance; make the best of it.' Oh, and here's the collection plate.

'They're not my kind of people'

Now, this is a difficult one. If you're a football fan, used to spending Saturdays in exaggerated yelling after a proper liquid build-up, then feeling you'd be in a minority on a Sunday morning in church is perfectly understandable. You would be. It's possible to parody the congregation in the way one feature writer did, noting that

> the churchgoers all look like the nicer characters in Australian soaps, a permanent half smile, slightly out of date inexpensive clothes. The guy next to me – he's not making much of a fashion statement. He's wearing a brownish jacket, grey trousers, has shortish hair . . . the women are wearing floral dresses to mid calf. I would bet there are no vegetarians in the house, or people who read philosophy, or tell really good jokes in bars. These churchgoers are people I never get to meet.[2]

What the casual visitor wouldn't immediately notice is that there may well be a professor of philosophy there, there will certainly be some vegetarians, and there are probably one or two saints in the congregation whose lives would make them gasp if they but knew. But – point taken; there is a tendency in the average congregation to grey hair, safe fashion, and (occasionally) some wonderful eccentricity.

'I don't understand what's going on'

I sometimes try to imagine what it would be like if I went to a pub where, on some hidden cue, a group of men, dressed in unusual and exotic gear, got up and walked solemnly round a table three times, then sat down, sang a curious snatch of music, and lapsed into silence. This would be followed by readings from some worthy but incomprehensible ancient text, and the strained singing of a communal dirge. If this kind of behaviour continued for an hour or so I might be rather glad to escape at the end and return to the normal world where I knew roughly what was going on. In a somewhat overstated way, this may be what it seems like to someone entering a church service for the first time. Even someone returning to church after some years' absence might well lament that they didn't know where they were in the service and felt they were in a strange, new land. The net result is that newcomers can feel embarrassed and out of place when they come to church. They don't know the rules, but the message is quite clear – this place isn't for them.

So let's not underestimate the problem of going to church for very many people in our society today. Some commentators point out that this is even more tragic since people are more aware of their spiritual needs now than for many years. Writing in *The Times*, Jane Shilling commented:

> It's strange that the C of E should find itself so beleaguered and diminished at a time when people, particularly the 18–30 group to whom it so desperately wants to 'reach out', are so articulate in expressing their feelings of spiritual need. The longing for spirituality is not just there in encrypted form – the feature pages' obsession with perfect bodies, perfect homes, perfect children and fuzzy mysticism – feng shui, yoga, fasting and the whole Ab Fab range of partially understood alternative spiritual disciplines. It is overt: our state of the art sound systems resonate to the sounds of chanting monks and nuns; we go on retreat to monasteries; we buy mousemats decorated with images of baby angels . . . spirituality, in short, is not a product like laceless trainers or isotonic sports drinks that we never knew we wanted. We want it, right enough. All the Church has to do is deliver. But it can't . . .[3]

Somehow the Church isn't making the connection. We assume that, deep down, people will want to come to church if we just make the odd adjustment here and there. The malaise is deeper. We've traded too long on goodwill; we've been rearranging the ecclesiastical furniture when people have been wanting God; we've often missed the cultural boat, watching it depart from our shores while we keep standing on the dockside in the illusory safety of the past.

However, one of the convictions behind this little book is that the Church is beginning to engage with the more profound questions of connectedness, and is grappling positively with issues of community, spirituality, cultural relevance, freedom to grow as human beings, and so on. In fact I believe that in many, many places the local church is in remarkably good shape. It just doesn't know it.

Moreover, hundreds of millions of people all over the world do go to church regularly and positively, week by week. They don't seem to suffer any ill effects. Indeed they often seem wonderfully liberated and energized by the experience. The question might just crop up in the minds of the curious – 'Is there something we're missing?'

2

Why is it worth going to church?

OK, so there are problems. Going to church is a risky business, fraught with tripwires and potential embarrassments. Nevertheless, it's one of the most common human activities in the world. In country after country churchgoing seems irresistible. There are 2,000 million people who identify with Jesus Christ and his way of life, and most of them go to church with some regularity. Why?

Because we're on a journey

It's like this: we're getting along fine, thank you very much. Education – tick. Job – tick. Life partner – tick. Housing – tick. Then something happens. It may be that it's the arrival of a child, or the death of a parent, or an encounter with illness, or the loss of a job, but something interrupts the smooth flow of personal progress. A crack appears in the concrete that has settled over our deeper lives, our questions about life, meaning and purpose. And through this crack a flower comes from nowhere. It needs to be investigated. Where shall we go to ask the right questions? Perhaps to church.

Many people see their lives as a journey. Indeed, the journey motif lies deep in the human psyche. Most people have a sense of moving on and encountering new stages with new questions and tasks. Jung said that the chief task of the second half of life is to find a spiritual meaning and interpretation of the life we're living. As we turn round the corner on this journey, there, almost inevitably, will be a church.

Because we're looking for a framework to live in

There are huge gains to be found in the freedom and honesty that characterize the early twenty-first century. The internet has set off an explosion of knowledge. New technologies bring the world to our living rooms and give us hope for all kinds of medical breakthroughs and other benefits. There is less hypocrisy, more openness and greater sensitivity to minorities. On the other hand, the exponential changes in every aspect of contemporary living have brought bewilderment and confusion to many of us as this 'future shock' reverberates through our lives. Living on the edge, as we do, brings with it the anxiety that we could tip over into primal chaos through climate change, biological and nuclear terrorism, nanotechnology that goes off the rails.

We face ethical questions daily of which earlier generations couldn't have conceived. In many ways we've outgrown our moral and spiritual strength. Many people, therefore, turn to the Church to find a framework of values, and habits of thought and action, that offer sanity in this spinning world. They aren't trying to escape; rather they're asking whether the ancient disciplines of the heart might not be mined afresh for a deeper wisdom to save us from individual and corporate shipwreck. It's happened before – every few centuries people discover the Church's faith afresh and wonder why nobody has ever told them about it.

Because it's a place of moral seriousness in a trivialized culture

Following on the above line of thought, many people grow weary of the absurd excesses of a culture that reduces everything – even serious discussion – to the level of entertainment. We are almost literally 'entertaining ourselves to death'. Ours is a culture where (judging by the money and media coverage involved) celebrity is more important than serious moral debate. Climate scientists tell us we're still drinking cocktails on the *Titanic* as the lifeboats are being launched. The newsstands are crowded with magazines giving us more details about the lives of B-list celebrities than we could possibly assimilate; meanwhile the ship sinks.

In this context, the Church can be a serious debater, offering thoughtful, measured and positive reflections on social and political issues. Not that everybody appreciates such contributions. Secularists want religion firmly excluded from the public arena, but most thinking people realize that the great faith traditions draw on ancient wisdom which cannot be ignored, and that religion and politics are inextricably mixed as they pursue the common good. Church, then, seems a good place to go to in order to be part of an important moral discourse. And anything is better than *Big Brother*!

Because churches make an honest attempt at community in a culture that's forgotten how to do it

As society fragments into ever tighter interest groups, church is one place where there's a genuine attempt to build a diverse, welcoming, all-age community which crosses the falsifying barriers of our common humanity and celebrates the fascinating variety of our human heritage. The fact that I have to see Edna Bucket as my sister in Christ or that I

sit in my pew alongside Walter Woebegone whose theo-
logical views I regard as off the wall, means that I'm having to
embody something that's essential to the well-being of society,
and even the future of humanity. We have to learn to live
together constructively on this crowded planet. In church
we meet people of all intellectual and social backgrounds;
we meet people who we would never otherwise encounter,
let alone share a meal with. We meet the high achiever, the
struggler, the notorious sinner and the occasional saint,
the activist and the contemplative, the youthful idealist and
the wizened warrior of forgotten battles. These are God's
people, who you can either see as God's wounded disciples
or the unlikely shock troops of the kingdom. Both are true.
They are no better and no worse than the rest of society –
but they are committed to each other, in community.

Bel Mooney, writing in the *Sunday Times* at Easter, asked:

> Does the Church matter? It does. 'This is our story, this is
> our song,' said the Revd Caroline Neill in the pulpit at the
> beginning of Holy Week. Looking around at babies in arms,
> oblivious toddlers scampering up the aisle, teenagers in jeans,
> the middle-aged, the elderly; contemplating the idea of
> sacrifice, hearing prayers for mercy and the injunction 'Go
> in peace', I realised two important things. First, I could not
> quarrel with anything in the message of the service. Second,
> that the feeling of community I took home with my palm
> cross represents far more than my neighbourhood here
> in Bath.[4]

When community works, it shows.

Because I'm a learner, and church seems to be a community of learners

At its best, the church knows it's a school for the learning
of an earthy holiness. There's an attractive humility about
such a church because it doesn't presume to have all the

answers in a neatly wrapped package with a silver bow, but to be a community of learners gathered around the life of Jesus. And these learners aren't taking copious notes and preparing for exams; they're watching and trying to imitate the Main Man. It's a process of formation, not information. It's 'learning Christ' as St Paul puts it (though he puts it in the negative, 'that is not the way you learned Christ': Ephesians 4.20). One of the earliest descriptions of the Christian faith was simply 'the Way', and those who go to church and call themselves Christians certainly fall off the Way regularly. The difference is, instead of lying in the ditch and cursing the slippery path, they climb back on to it again and keep going. Make no mistake – Christians don't claim moral superiority; Jesus said, 'I have come to call not the righteous but sinners to repentance' (Luke 5.32). And repentance is a lifelong process. We'll be learners to the end.

Because the building talks a different language, and it's fascinating

This is the opposite of one of the reasons for not going to church in the previous chapter. Here the church is a positive magnet, drawing people into its deep rhythms and its silent music. What communicates here is hard to put into words. It's just the place, the history, the prayers and dreams that have gone into it, the hopes and fears of all the years – and sometimes the sheer space. In our crowded lives, space is hard to find. Space to think or stop thinking, space to reflect, space to rest, to be still, to be . . . Churches are past masters at this. They offer non-judgemental space for us to sift our experiences and sort out our dilemmas. They cleanse us. On a good day, with a following wind, they may even leave us feeling embraced, understood, loved. Churches can do all this without a word of worship being spoken. Hidden in this paragraph, of course, is a mute plea that churches be left open, every day, so that folk can creep in quietly and touch the edge of eternity.

Because I might strike lucky

I may get a really interesting sermon from a thoughtful priest who obviously cares about ideas, listens to what's going on in the world, and tries to make some sense of it all; and who obviously cares about God. There aren't many contexts today where you can hear a careful, well informed and imaginative conversation between the wisdom of God in the Bible and the experience of human beings in the world. If we have preachers who are 'willing to risk body, blood, wealth and honour to preach' (Martin Luther) and who really care about how people can flourish in today's world (and who also know a thing or two about communication), then we can have in the sermon a truly enlivening, even life-changing, experience. And if it's not always like that, there's always next week!

Because I want to get in touch with God

Got there at last! I didn't want to assume too much, but this is the heart of it. The writer Julian Barnes started a Lent talk on Radio 4 in 2008 by saying: 'I don't believe in God, but I miss him.' Many people are in that position today, but some of them want to go a step further and see if they can actually get in touch with the elusive Stranger. They might even have some instinct that the psychiatrist in Peter Shaffer's play *Equus* was right when he said: 'If you don't worship you'll shrink; it's as brutal as that.' Reluctantly, perhaps, they might come to church because God might be there.

For others, worship is as natural as breathing. Mike Riddell writes:

For those whose hearts have been shafted with love, worship is as natural and as unavoidable as a tree coming into blossom with the warmth of spring. It is love language . . . The truth about us humans is that we have been made from love, and it is only in love that we discover what we are. Like a caged bird returned to the air, worship releases us into our natural environment, and we discover that we can swoop and soar and dive.[5]

Worship isn't for sycophants who seek to buy off a narcissistic God with constant affirmation; it's for people who seek to live the truth of their nature as made by God, in God, and for God – who is Love.

Because when times are hard, there are resources to be found there

You don't have to be strong all the time. The myth of constant success is a hard myth to live by but we often spend our lives trying to ascend the ladders that society puts before us. Sometimes we just run out of puff and need to sit down at the bottom of the ladder and recuperate and reassess. Strangely that's often when we encounter Christ who came down the ladder in the incarnation, and who now sits with those who can't climb any more. Churches can be places of rest, companionship and restoration. And if forgiveness needs to be part of the deal, the Church specializes in that too.

Because there's a saint or two to be found in there, and saints are exciting

Most of us are just a shadow of our future selves, and it's good to get a glimpse of what a human being is meant to be.

3

What is the Church for?

I'm going to set the bar quite high here. The primary task of the Church is to worship. We come to church for all sorts of reasons, some of which hardly bear repeating in respectable company, but the Church itself, the Church as a whole, the Church in its pure, uncut form, is there to worship God. We may be there because we like the vicar, want the baby baptized ('christened', your mother-in-law called it), made a bargain with God while in hospital, want little Joel to go to a church school, just got the feeling we ought to, lost the toss – all sorts of reasons.

But there's no getting away from it: worship is about God, not us. Hard as it is to tear ourselves away from the narcissistic mirror, worship is meant to be the moment of truth when the One who we might have dimly remembered through the week blazes into full focus. In worship we celebrate God, the Source of life. It's the time in the week when we get it right for once, when we let God be God and dethrone our idols, chief of which is our own ego. Worship is what we exist for. I worship; therefore I am.

Now, this could come across as a somewhat worrying idea. Does this suggest that God is an immature despot who needs constant congratulations to keep himself going, a B-list celebrity who can't exist without fawning fans? Absolutely not! We need to worship in order to find out who we truly are. Worship is for *our* health, not God's. St Augustine said: 'O God, you have made us for yourself, and our souls are restless until they find their rest in you.' We are worshipping beings, but if we deflect our worship on to those things that are not God, then we change the value of everything, swap the price tickets on every item in the store, and 'worship the creature and not the Creator'. That way lies self-destruction.

Moreover, we worship not just for ourselves but for the whole world, in order to keep the world on course. We'll never have everyone coming to church on Sunday morning, not should we expect them to. We worship on their behalf, holding them and all the things they do, before God. It's a huge privilege.

All this means that the *form* of worship isn't as important as the *fact* of worship. The acid test is whether an act of worship is truly alive and life-giving, not whether it's liturgically perfect. A Christian from South America had visited England and was invited to tell a meeting back home what had impressed him about the Church in Britain. He replied: 'All the services start punctually. Even if the Spirit hasn't arrived yet!' It's the Spirit who gives life to worship. What matters is not what form of words we use but that our spirits are ignited by divine fire. Wherever the worship goes and whatever its shape, what really matters is that we catch the tail of the divine tiger, and hold on.

Where worship starts

Worship starts in human wonder and ends in holy obedience. It starts with an awakening of the sleeping beauty of our wonder at the sheer miracle of life. It's the 'isness' of things that sometimes stops us in our tracks. A child, freshly minted from the womb, a leaf on the turn, a friendship beyond words, a mountain scraping the sky. The poet Rilke said: 'One thing, truly experienced, even once, is enough for a lifetime.' All this wonder we can bring into worship in our own church, so that we are in the frame of mind to encounter the even greater wonder that is Jesus Christ. But how can we pour infinity into a pint pot?

As we get caught up in worship we find that it's a kind of glad shout of celebration, like the 'Yes' on our lips when our side scores a goal, or the 'Yes' in our heart when the last note of the symphony echoes around the concert hall. It's the 'Yes' we feel when we fall in love and we'd do anything for the one we love. Worship is our 'Yes' to life and to God, in the midst of many voices that tell us to keep quiet or to keep our preferences to ourselves. It's a shout of exhilaration and gratitude.

That's the theory anyway. The reality can be rather different. On a wet Sunday morning in February when there's a pile of work to be done and the sun hasn't shone since 1966, it's often hard to raise a 'Yes'. 'If you say so', or 'Whatever' feels nearer the mark. Nevertheless, making the effort to put ourselves into a place of glad gratitude is nearly always worthwhile. It changes our point of view. It says: 'This is what I was made for. This is where I'm meant to be.' And gradually, oh so gradually, we become a fraction more like the one we worship. It's always like that. As Tom Wright puts it:

> Those who worship money become, eventually, human calculating machines. Those who worship sex become obsessed with their own attractiveness or prowess. Those who worship power become more and more ruthless.[6]

But those who worship Jesus Christ become, all unaware, more and more like him, though very slowly, in small gradations. And the world needs them.

Of course there are all sorts of strange practices that we experience in worship. The dress code is one, in Anglican churches at least. As a bishop I wear a mitre at special services. At one such service I heard a little girl say to her mother, 'Mummy, is that man a chef?' But special clothes help to make it a special occasion. We aren't just popping down to the shops; we're meeting the Lord of Hosts. Moreover, rituals develop in order to mark special situations, whether that be a wedding, a cup final, a funeral, or a graduation. We are ritual-making people. It's worth taking time to find out why church practices in worship, and elsewhere, have developed as they have.

Soul food

If worship starts in human wonder, it ends in holy obedience. But in between there's a journey, and that journey takes in, primarily, Scripture and sacrament, undergirded by prayer. Scripture is soul food, and sacrament is soul music. Let's see what that means.

We need *soul food* to eat, regularly. The Bible was written by many hands over a period of a thousand years and is a distinctly diverse and complex set of writings, comprising history and ancient tales, wise sayings and prayers, poetry and rules of the road, warnings and wild dreams, letters, and that strange new *genre* 'Gospels'. But through it all, people hear God speaking to them, and always have. This is the word made readable, which points us to the Word made flesh (Jesus).

Of course we have to navigate deep, disturbing waters on the way. Why did God have it in for the Amalekites? Is the rape of Tamar by her half-brother suitable material for public reading? When Jael hammered a tent peg through Sisera's head, was that done to the glory of God? It's all lively stuff, and indeed it's all for us to work on even when we don't understand it or are puzzled by it. Through the extraordinarily diverse narratives of Scripture we taste the huge variety of dishes which together give the full and balanced diet of soul food on which the world has feasted for centuries. One theologian called the Bible 'food for wrestlers'. Equally it's food for scholars, for seekers, for lovers and for simple followers. I expect to be grappling with the profound complexity of the Bible till the end of my life.

Soul music

The sacrament of Holy Communion takes us into the world of *soul music*. I don't mean literal music; I mean that here in the sacrament are gifts that make the heart sing. Christ comes to us through bread and wine. We need symbols to encounter God because we couldn't stand the full charge of divine electricity without protection. Bread and wine are the ordinary, innocent things that Jesus chose as the means by which to give us his life. He promised this at the last supper he had with his friends. Now he calls *us* his friends as well (John 15.15), and shares his inexhaustible life with us. I can't think of a greater privilege.

And this service of Holy Communion, or the Mass, or the Eucharist or the Lord's Supper, has fascinated and empowered millions of Christians ever since that first shared meal on a dark night in Jerusalem. It was a sad song the disciples sang that night, but after the amazing events of Easter, Ascension and Pentecost, that song has gone out into all the world as the victory song of the people of God – truly 'soul music' for the Church. I've sung that music on a mountainside in Scotland with the wind flapping the tent door to reveal glory outside and glory inside. I've sung it under a solitary tree in a wide, burning basin in the Sinai desert on Low Sunday, enjoying 'Thine be the Glory' and sharing the Peace with four bemused Bedouin. I've sung it at the high altar in Canterbury Cathedral, and by my father's deathbed, in a caravan in the south of France, and by the Sea of Galilee with water lapping my feet. And never better than on a thousand Sundays in ordinary parishes in Birmingham, Somerset, Durham, Canterbury and Oxford with the faithful people of God.

And always the question I ask myself is the one posed by the former Archbishop of Canterbury Michael Ramsey: 'The supreme question is not what we make of the Eucharist, but what the Eucharist is making of us.' How are we being made into people who make things change? How effectively are we singing the Lord's song in a strange land?

The 'end' of worship

This is where 'holy obedience' makes its appearance as the trajectory of worship. Certainly worship is about God, for God and to God. It starts with holy wonder and takes a path through Scripture and sacrament to the very heart of God's love for the world. But eventually it has to emerge in people who have been changed by the encounter. Then we're ready to set off into the thick of everyday life where people struggle to survive, to cope, to laugh, to thrive. Our task is to join in with God's great project of making a new world out of the debris of the old. We have to give him the best raw materials ('debris') we can provide. We offer all of ourselves to all God has revealed himself to be, for the sake of all we know of the world.

And it's our worship that keeps us on course.

4

So you're going (back) to church

So you're going to give it a go. It's a brave decision. There's a hint of countercultural courage about it. You fear that people have started going to church and never been seen again – not in ordinary life anyway. They've been lost in an ecclesiastical subculture, giving up *EastEnders* for the church council meeting. There may be something dangerously addictive here. You need to know more. So what are you likely to find?

The village church

In many respects a service here is little changed from when you last went – if you did. There's the same evocative, musty smell, and the same two ladies bustling about getting everything ready, while the organist is sorting out the music and trying out a few of the tunes. However, on your way in, you noticed in the porch a picture of a four-person 'Ministry Team', whatever that is, and one smiling face with the caption 'Your local priest' and an address in the neighbouring village. You're given a hymn book and a booklet and left to sit anywhere. It's not going to be difficult to find a seat. The service proceeds with rustic informality. More people seem to be involved in leading the worship these days – it isn't a one-person monologue. And there's been some innovation too – there's a quieter water heater for the coffee, although it's still been heating up and cutting out ever since the Peace. The weekly news sheet shows there are lots of activities going on across this cluster of parishes: training for worship leaders, a Christian learning course on 'Tough Questions', and a meeting on climate change to be held in the biggest of the six villages.

And there seems to be a new children's weeknight club called 'The Riot Act' (it doesn't augur well, you think . . .). Nevertheless, things have moved on. It may even be for the better.

The town centre church

Here too a lot seems reasonably familiar. There are three morning services. A quiet, said Communion at 8 a.m., using the old form of service; then at 9.30 there's something called Family Worship, and at 11.15 there's Holy Communion with a robed choir. It seems that consumer choice has reached church worship too. There's a busy, purposeful feel to the church on Sunday morning – a smart news bulletin, new hymn books and a projection screen displaying 'Welcome to St Andrew's'. A music group is tuning up and then starts playing some soft gospel songs as more and more people fill up the seats (no pews now).

There's also a feeling of doors having been opened to the wider community – there are prayers for the appointment of a new head teacher at the local school, and prayers too for newcomers on the estate being built on the edge of the town. The notices speak of home groups, a teddy bears' picnic, and a Leadership Team, and there also seems to be what's called a 'church plant' happening at the school (the mind boggles). There's clearly a lot going on. You notice especially an appeal for soft furnishings for a new prayer room which they hope will be open all day with resources and artefacts, music, icons, books, candles (dangerous) and lots of ideas for how to pray. Clearly spirituality is at the heart of what they do here. Maybe it's worth a return visit.

The suburban church

It has to be admitted that the building doesn't quicken the pulse. The worthy 1960s' architecture leaves the church plain but open and with a strange, squeaky floor surface. The gallant congregation look to have grown gracefully old together. But their welcome is warm. Someone is setting up a Traidcraft stall to sell fairly traded goods, and someone else a stall selling recycled Christmas cards in aid of the hospice. At five to ten the priest flies in and attaches herself to the five-strong choir. They clearly try to involve both young (a nine-year-old in Day-Glo trainers) and old (three servers, somewhat underemployed). The sermon hits the spot by holding together the week's news and the day's Scripture readings. People really seem to know and enjoy each other and yet they're eager to welcome a newcomer. Full marks for effort this time. You leave with a small spring in your step, although you're not sure if you've met with God or just the people of God.

The 'high' church

It looks quite forbidding at first. You pass the traumatic crucifix outside and enter a large Victorian building with a hushed atmosphere and a faint sweet smell in the air. There's also an air of quiet expectancy as you wait in the pew for something to happen, watching the white-robed servers preparing the sanctuary, always bowing as they pass the altar. There are statues of a wan-looking Mary, mother of Jesus. Then a bell is rung, the organ strikes up and the procession winds its way through the church led by a man and a boy swinging a pot on a chain (a thurible, you find out later) which wafts out incense.

The service is formal, highly ordered theatre. It obviously matters to people, and they know what to do, so although it's all a bit of a mystery for a newcomer, it's somehow a good mystery. There's a sense of 'otherness', something completely different and yet profoundly important. When it's over, the congregation seem to relax visibly and laughter fills the back of the church where good coffee and chocolate biscuits are served. Conversation is surprisingly normal, considering the highly esoteric experience you've just shared, and there's genuine warmth. As you leave, you think to yourself that this may not be life as we know it, but there's definitely something going on here.

The cathedral

The service ought to have a kite mark: 'Quality assured'. It's part sacred concert, part sacred theatre, in which the building has a major non-speaking part. This is seriously good worship, with everything from the sermon to the silverware on the altar being of the highest standard. There's a comfortable feeling of being able to play hide-and-seek with God in a place like this. No one is going to accost you; there certainly won't be any spiritual SATs assessment. You could come here for sheer aesthetic pleasure – but you might find yourself starting to believe. Nothing too extreme, of course; they don't do enthusiasm here, nor will there be much likelihood of revival breaking out. But minds will be stimulated, artistic senses will be nourished, and people might well inch closer to a personal relationship with God (not that they'd call it that, of course). Five for artistic impression; five for content; one for welcome.

The church plant

Now what was that strange-sounding image? A 'church plant' – which has nothing to do with eccentric horticulture but everything to do with growing a new church. It meets in a school hall where the 'church' has clearly had to be set up afresh this and every Sunday morning. It feels odd and yet reassuring to come into a familiar place and see unfamiliar objects – a cross, a scattering of tea-light candles, banners, music band, PA system, etc. The atmosphere is totally relaxed; the worship leader (is he ordained?) isn't wearing any robes, there's no procession, no choir, no stained-glass window. (Oh, come on! What do you expect?) But what the service lacks in recognizable rituals it makes up for in sheer enthusiasm, genuineness and noise.

Children run around the wooden floor before being swept off to their Junior Church activities in nearby rooms. Suddenly you're left in a quieter space with a preacher who speaks straight from heart to heart – though if your heart is somewhere else at the time you can feel pretty detached from it all. As you drink coffee and are run into by an enthusiastic three-year-old, you reflect that this isn't a place that specializes in the numinous, but it certainly does specialize in Jesus.

The 'fresh expression'

They call it 'alternative worship' and it's certainly no Matins. The lights are atmospherically low; there's a drink to take to a comfortable low chair; soft music plays. The worship is about to explore the theme of forgiveness. There's a striking mix of film clips, poetry, mood music, structured chat, projected images, participative prayer with various optional activities, a 'cool down' period. It's full of imagination, although a bit threatening for those of a nervous disposition. Not a huge number there, but seems like a high level of personal investment from quite a few, and the age profile is encouragingly 30s. Friendly, non-precious chat afterwards. A number of midweek opportunities for practical social action, workshops, concerts etc. are projected on to the big screens. Seems like a thoughtful, accessible community. Next week perhaps?

5

Making the most of the service

So we're going to church. What are we going to find when we get there, and how can we get the most out of it? Already that's a questionable question! It isn't 'what we can get out of it' that matters but Who we encounter in it, and that depends on how much we enter into the whole experience. I've already pointed out that we can easily slip into seeing a church service as Christian entertainment. That isn't really our fault. It's the default mode for our leisure-soaked culture that when we go somewhere special we expect to be entertained.

It has to be admitted that if the worship of the average Sunday morning service is put into the same bracket as our sophisticated entertainment industry, it might not come out too well. The temperature of the church breaches health and safety regulations. The choir does its best but it's hardly going to win *X Factor*. The lesson reader struggles with some dark corner of the Old Testament and loses on points. The sermon is acceptable but it has no sound bites and there isn't an autocue. At the end of the service you've survived, but you're not really sure what it was all about.

The key is to approach the service in a quite different way. We are here to place ourselves before the majestic, loving Creator of everything there is. It's actually a privilege just to be here. What we are entering is a sacred event which needs our active participation and our eager expectation. Think of it like this:

Before the service

I occasionally wonder if some of us slip into a pew, kneel quietly, count to ten and then get up again, job done. That may be a libel. However, I wonder whether we couldn't develop a greater sense of holy anticipation before the service? As we worship we're theoretically bringing all of ourselves to all God has shown himself to be, so perhaps we could use the time sitting quietly before the service to reflect on the past week, its high and low points, and then, metaphorically, 'take our life in our hands' and place it before God. The attitude we could foster might be what we feel before a concert starts, when the orchestra is in place, they've tuned up, the lights are lowered, the opening applause has died down, the conductor raises his baton, and . . .

Hymns and songs

Music styles in worship are the subject of many books and even more arguments. A composer was once being criticized by a woman for his modern hymns. The woman said: 'I think God deserves our best.' 'Yes, certainly,' he said, 'and that *is* my best.' 'Best' comes in many forms; our task is to enter it and give it our best too. That will mean making a conscious effort to think about the words we're singing. I often come to the last verse of a hymn and realize to my alarm that I haven't taken in a word; I've just been singing a tune (with words attached). Our hymns and songs contain wonderful expressions of Christian truth, great poetry, evocative ideas, exciting promises, deep reassurance – and some dross. But even the dross was written from the heart and deserves to be sung from the heart (and mind, if possible). Of course, if they sing a hymn you know to a tune you don't know, all promises are off; you're entitled to get mad!

Bible readings

It's easy to feel we've entered a thick, dark jungle when we get to the Bible readings, particularly the Old Testament. To make sense of some of the passages we could do with a lot more background knowledge than most of us come with, and some fairly sophisticated tools of interpretation. People talk about 'the plain meaning of the text' but that can often be profoundly elusive. Nevertheless the people who compiled the lectionary of Sunday readings or chose the readings for the sermon series clearly had our welfare at heart, and in any case the sermon is still to come and will hopefully tackle the tricky bits.

But let's put first things first: when we listen to the Bible we aren't just hearing a few useful thoughts from ancient literature – we're being dealt with by God. Mahatma Gandhi said: 'You Christians look after a document containing enough dynamite to blow all civilisations to pieces, turn the world upside down, and bring peace to a battle-torn planet. But you treat it as though it is nothing more than a piece of literature.'[7] The trick then is not to disengage the brain as we go through the comforting ritual of sitting down to listen to the readings. Resist the mental temptation to wander off immediately to the afternoon's televised football match, the annoying problem you haven't resolved at work, or the tax form waiting on the kitchen table. Glorious things are being spoken. Active listening is demanding, but it's hugely rewarding.

The sermon

Years of sermons have inoculated some churchgoers against the importance of what is about to take place. This is the time when the *spoken word* is hopefully being faithful to the *written word* in order to lead us to the *living Word*, who is Jesus Christ himself. Unfortunately experience seems to have left many people sceptical about the sermon. I even heard my own wife whisper to our small daughter as I climbed into the pulpit on one occasion: 'All right. You can go to sleep now.'

Ouch! As we listen to a sermon it's helpful if we can think of it as a kind of three-way conversation between God, the preacher and ourselves. We listen out for God's personal word to us, we think our questions, we make our resolutions – in other words, we participate in, and even *co-create*, the sermon. We will always be in both agreement and disagreement with a sermon; what matters is what God is saying to us if we'll listen *internally* as well as externally. The preacher is speaking 'in the name of God', and that needs to be taken seriously by both preacher and listener. Preaching looks easier than it actually is, but it remains true that it's easier to *preach* five sermons than it is to *live* one. And living that one is our task.

Prayers

Who knows what goes on in the darkness when eyes are closed and minds set free? The temptation again is for minds to go walkabout. Alternatively we might find ourselves irritated by the sugary tone of voice of the person leading the prayers, or the way he or she tells God what's happening, or the implied political slant, or the choice of things we pray about or don't pray about, or the silence we keep or don't keep, and so on. Almost anything can lead us to switch off in protest or tune out in boredom. Please resist this temptation. The spoken prayers are only jumping-off points for our spirits to reach out to the loving Spirit of God with heartfelt thanks and prayers of need. Try to be truly focused on lifting these people and places right into the heart of God, loving them enough to be serious in your praying. As we do that, we may find ourselves bearing some of the pain alongside those people whose lives have been shattered by the latest atrocity of war or the latest sweep of starvation in Africa, just as we find ourselves emotionally drained when we watch a film that draws us deeply into the tragedy of the plot or the pain of the characters.

Prayer is an opportunity to rejoice with those who rejoice and weep with those who weep. How often do we pray to the point of tears? The prayers are not another time for us to be a literary or spiritual critic, judging performance and style. It's a time for deep, personal engagement with the realities of human life, in which we hold together the needs of the world and the endless love of God. It's good if we rise from prayer exhausted!

Holy Communion

In many churches this will be the central focus of the service, whether it's called the Mass, the Eucharist, the Lord's Supper, or the Jesus meal. This is where actions speak louder than words, and receiving bread and wine as a way of receiving Christ's life into ours is an action more powerful than any other in Christian experience. 'Take and eat this in remembrance that Christ died for you' – this is the action that has always most characterized Christians as they gather together. We remember and re-inhabit the death and resurrection of Jesus. We anticipate the heavenly banquet. We receive Christ. It's therefore the most moving part of the service, and we shouldn't skip lightly to take Communion, but rather approach thoughtfully and expectantly. One way of thinking about the act of taking Communion is that when we open our hands, we hold in them all our experiences, problems, relationships, hopes and decisions, and offer them to God's gracious handling. We also bring the emptiness of our hearts so that they can be filled with the life, goodness and energy of Christ. What an exchange – new for old, fullness for emptiness, joy for confusion, life for death. We come away from receiving Communion with full and thankful hearts. We might sometimes, of course, be going up to receive Communion quite at odds with God or with someone else. That's still all right; we're going to receive God's help with the dilemma. God is always the giver. Sometimes, of course, we may feel we're going through the motions, or we may be too aware of the mechanics of getting to the right place in the line, and kneeling down without falling over, and holding the cup without spilling it, to be thinking any 'holy thoughts'. No matter. Remember that it's what God is doing here that matters, not what we may be feeling about it. Christ is the host at this meal and he's the one who's giving his life away. 'Be still, for the presence of the Lord, the Holy One, is here.' If we are not confirmed, it's still absolutely right to go up to receive a blessing. God is always wanting to bless us. And perhaps we might then talk to the priest about confirmation!

Blessing and dismissal

In most churches we are offered God's blessing, his gift of well-being, at the end of the service. It's a final and beautiful act. And then we're sent out to get on with it – the loving and serving and changing the world. As is sometimes said – 'The worship has ended; now the *service* begins.' However, it's worthwhile not to leap up immediately to collar someone you really need to see (or to escape from the person you really want to avoid). We might just want to sit quietly for a moment to reflect on what gifts we have received in the service, the insights, the encouragement, the moments of pleasure. We might pledge to 'take the service home', to take Sunday into Monday and live out our worship in our lives. Then off we go to coffee – and perhaps to talk to someone we don't know.

Not every service we go to will seem to be an epoch-making event, but gradually, I can assure you, we are changed.

6

Mind the gap

I have to admit in the midst of all my encouragement to people to try going to church or keep going to it, that there's still a danger of disappointment. There's still a gap between hope and reality. In this chapter I want to warn you to 'mind the gap'. Bishop John V. Taylor encouraged his 20+-year-old son to come with him to church one Sunday morning. Afterwards the son said he didn't think he'd be going again. 'Why?' asked his father. 'Well,' he said, 'at one level everything was fine. The vicar said all the right things, but the trouble is he wasn't saying them *to* anybody. He didn't listen, and it didn't seem to occur to him to do so.'

I fear there's still a chance we may not be blown away by our visits to church. So here are some points to remember.

1 *There's no perfect church.* As the old line goes – if you find the perfect church, don't join it, because you'll ruin it. There's no such thing as a perfect church, because we're all flawed human beings. We bring our own confusions and wounds, and if you multiply those by the number of people in church, you've got quite a potential for disaster. Be gentle with the wounded body of Christ, as you would like the body of Christ to be gentle with you.

2 *Churches are for belonging, not tasting.* You understand the Church and its story best when you look through

the stained-glass windows from the inside. From in here you glimpse the glory of faith and you appreciate the depth of the tradition of worship, witness and service. You also meet the strange, motley band of fellow pilgrims God has given you, and you learn about the movement of God in their lives. And occasionally you find yourself having tea with a saint.

3 *Go and talk to the vicar, priest, minister or pastor.* Introduce yourself and ask for a chat. Tell him or her about your journey so far, your doubts and commitments. See if there is a particular kind of engagement with the church which may be best for you – an introductory or nurture course perhaps, or a form of practical service, one of the services rather than another, and so on. If the vicar or priest is worth his or her salt, this would be a refreshing and important encounter, trying to help you on your journey.

4 *Some seekers and searchers find cathedrals or other large churches good places in which to start.* By their size and relatively impersonal nature, they allow people to play hide-and-seek with God, giving them space to soak up the presence of God without pressure to sign up for the summer outing or become churchwarden. One of our greatest needs is to provide 'third spaces' (neither church nor home) where people can explore, reflect, observe for a while, and then approach in their own time. Once commitment makes sense, of course, cathedrals can provide wonderfully rich worship and fellowship as well.

5 *Don't tar every church with the same brush.* This church may not be right for you, but that doesn't mean every church is hopeless. I'm not advocating endless church-hopping to find the best deal you can get: that's one of the more tedious aspects of our consumerist culture. Nevertheless, churches have very different characters. One interesting approach was worked out by an anthropologist theologian named James Hopewell and, using his professional skills of 'participant observation', he

constructed a grid of churches based on their dominant character traits.[8] He found that churches tend to have a distinctive 'character', or rather they negotiate between a number of character types, with one or two usually being dominant. One consequence is that they tend to attract people with similar character types; they find they 'fit in'. Another consequence is that those who bring a different character to the party tend to stand out as 'radical', 'difficult', or simply 'different'. The character types he identifies are:

Gnostic: (Not a brilliant use of this technical word.) This type of church moves forward steadily, believing little is accomplished by radical change or unusual beliefs and practices. God's good Spirit can be trusted to bring about progress over time. The natural rhythms of the church's life can be enhanced, but the basic framework continues to be effective. God works through and alongside his people, and much can be achieved, given time. You might just recognize many solid Church of England congregations in this description. There's a sanity and balance here that still achieves much over time to the glory of God.

Canonic: Churches of this 'character' take tradition as their starting point – a tradition resting either on the Bible or on the Church. There is considerable reliance on 'authority' and the church will not move far without being quite clear that either 'the Bible teaches' or 'the Church says' that it's all right to do so. The lines are more clearly drawn in a 'canonic' church. People know where they are and feel pretty comfortable in that context.

Charismatic: Churches of this type are open to change as the Holy Spirit guides. Whom the Spirit guides and what the Spirit is actually saying may be more contentious, but there's a readiness to act in new ways because God is alive, active and expected. The supernatural dimension of life is assumed in a way a gnostic church would find perplexing, and the experiential dimension of faith is assumed in a way a canonic church would find questionable. However, with an openness to the Spirit come risks of interpretation and the possibility of conflict.

Empiric: This type of church is built on the virtues of common sense and pragmatism. Facts are facts, and God is to be found in them. Members of this kind of church are probably happy that other churches and other believers are different, but they are quite clear that the further reaches of charismatic or canonic churches are not for them or (they would beg to suggest) for other rational, open-minded people. Typical phrases heard at a Parochial Church Council would be, 'Let's face facts', 'That sounds a bit far-fetched', and (famously) 'Is it in the budget?'

This typology of churches can be very helpful in coming to understand why you may not have felt 'at home' in one church but you did feel 'in your element' in another. In any particular church people tend to think about issues facing them and their church in ways that are similar to each other, and to be just a little uncomfortable with those who approach issues differently. However, there's great value in having at least some people of different character type in the church to provide the abrasion and internal critique. They keep the church leadership on its toes, and in a sense represent the views of the wider Church in the midst of the local church.

All this adds up to a plea not to give up on the whole Church because of problems you might have with a particular church. The people of God are gloriously diverse and they gather together in an extraordinary variety of ways.

And if all else fails, remember that God is infinitely bigger than his Church. Keep in touch with the Lord of Life, and in due course some form of church will emerge which is right for you.

Notes

1 Antony Flew, *There is a God* (New York: HarperOne, 2007).
2 William Leith, *Independent on Sunday*, 1992.
3 Jane Shilling, *The Times*, 2001.
4 Bel Mooney, *Sunday Times*, March 2006.
5 Mike Riddell, *Godzone* (Oxford: Lion, 1992, p. 91).
6 Tom Wright, *Simply Christian* (London: SPCK, 2006, p.127).
7 Mahatma Gandhi, source unknown.
8 James F. Hopewell, *Congregation* (Philadelphia, PA: Fortress Press/London: SCM Press, 1987).

Further reading

Here is a short list of books that can guide you further in your exploration of the topics discussed in this book.

The text of *Why Go to Church?* is drawn from chapters 1, 2, 3, 10, 15 and 17 of the author's *Going to Church: A user's guide* (SPCK, 2009). For more information on that book visit: www.spck.org.uk

Other books of related interest (all published by SPCK):

Jane Maycock, *God, Church, etc.: What you need to know* (2013)

John Pritchard, *God Lost and Found* (2011)

John Pritchard, *Living Faithfully: Following Christ in everyday life* (2013)

John Pritchard, *Beginning Again on the Christian Journey* (2014)

John Pritchard, *Ten: Why Christianity makes sense* (2014)

Rowan Williams, *Being Christian: Baptism, Bible, Eucharist, prayer* (2014)

Tom Wright, *Simply Christian* (2011)

Tom Wright, *The Meal Jesus Gave Us: Understanding Holy Communion* (2014)